From Bad
To Verse

From Bad To Verse

A COLLECTION OF MISSIONARY LIGHT VERSE

WRITTEN BY **BRUCE CALL**

ILLUSTRATED BY VAL CHADWICK BAGLEY

To Elders Bergin, Johnson, Baldi,
Pinkston, Peirson, Neff, and Waldie.

The CALL

There I was, on the porch,
When the mailman arrived.
It had been two whole weeks,
I had somehow survived.

He held back the letter,
Then on me he took pity,
He forked the thing over . . .
It was from Salt Lake City!

My fingers were clammy,
My palms drenched in sweat.
Would I go to Tahiti?
Or only Tibet?

Perhaps California
Would be more my style.
Or maybe the East,
Like New York or Rhode Isle.

The mainland of China
Would not be too bad.
Or Paris. Or Munich.
Or Egypt. Or Chad.

The world's full of places
I'm dying to see.
To serve in Helsinki'd
Be OK with me.

The moment had come.
I tore open the paper.
I swallowed my gum.
Where would I labor?

I unfolded the letter,
No taste in my mouth,
"You are here called to serve
In Galapagos, South."

Galapagos, South?!
With the terns and the tor-
toise?
Where what natives there are
Still use pestle and mortise?

I'll bleach and I'll crack
In the hot tropic sun,
As my girlfriends back home
Marry off, one by one.

I had to say something!
I opened my mouth . . .
When the Spirit said some-
thing:
"Galapagos, South."

Well, if that's where he wants
me,
Then that's where I'll be!
And the terns, and the tor-
toise,
Each Galapagosee,
Had better repent
When I open my mouth,
And humbly convert you,
Galapagos, South!

5 A.M. Blues

Angel Moroni, come blow your horn,
We're off to save thousands this glorious morn.
But where's my companion, to help save these sheep?
He's under the *Ensign*, fast asleep.

The Know-it-all Who Does

I've spoken fluent Russian since the sixth or seventh grade.
I can name each music masterpiece that's e'er been sung or played.
I read the Coptic languages, and hieroglyphs as well.
I calculate long formulas as fast as I can spell.

Now I've been called to Iowa, and more than all, I know
That though I could go anywhere, that's where I'm supposed to go.

Search the Scriptures

Whenever I think of the Great Beyond
Something occurs to me:
How will I locate the Pearly Gates
When I can't find Philippians 3?

A Day in the MTC

Awake. Mistake.
Glower. Shower.
Pray.

Renewed. Food.
Study. Everybody.
Pray.

Teach. Preach.
Lunch. Munch.
Pray.

Memorize. Synthesize.
Enunciate. Pronunciate.
Pray.

Learn. Yearn.
Beat. Eat.
Pray.

Read. Need.
Reap. Sleep.
Pray.

Missionary Limerick #1

In Seattle, an Elder named Brown
Always wore a perpetual frown.
"Let a smile," said one fella,
"Be your constant umbrella."
"Around here," he replied, "I would drown."

Insomniac's Prayer

Now I lay me down to sleep,
I pray my companion safe to keep.
Don't let a stranger sneak on in
And shave his head or wax his chin.
Let no invader gag his mouth,
Or stuff his nose with sauerkraut,
Or hide his glasses on the shelf.
If he snores again, I'll do it myself.

15

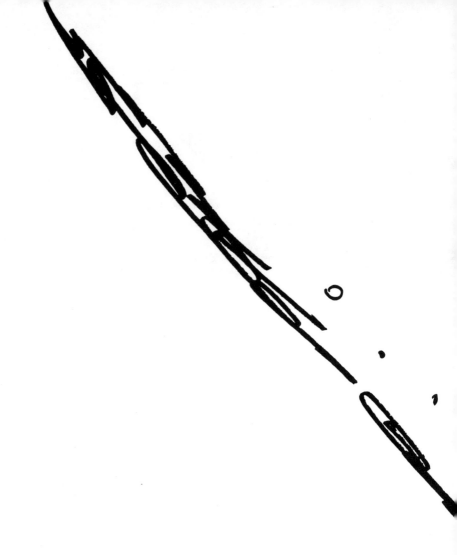

A Warning to Infidels and Pedestrians

The Kingdom of Heaven! Roll forth it will,
Like a big, fat Elder on a bike, downhill.
And like with the Elder, remember that
If you try to stop the Kingdom, you'll get squashed flat.

Just Lucky, I Guess

First there was the little dog
(he hid behind a boulder)
Then there was the bigger dog
(this scar, on my left shoulder)
Then the one that wouldn't let go
(his eyes were kinda yellow)
Last, the dog that barked a lot
("Down boy! Whoa! Down big fellow!")

Now, I've done a lot of fishin' from Bermuda to Cape May,
But not until my mission d' I get four bites in just one day.

Sister Missionaries

Oh the poor old Sisters! You gotta pity 'em!
They're the lowliest creatures on any meridian.
They look up to us with awe in their eyes.
They wonder and quake at our spiritual size.
They yearn for the day to our level they'll climb!
But they out-convert us, every time.

The President

If the President says, "Go jump in a lake,"
I'll find a lake and do it.
If the President says, "Convert the town,"
I'll say there's nothing to it.
If the President says, "Stand up and speak,"
Then I will have no fear.
If the President says, "Good job. Go home,"
I'll say, "Please, one more year?"

Vital Statistics

I used to recite the weight and size
Of the Forty-niners. RBI's
And stolen bases of major leaguers.
ERA's of the top relievers.
Shooting percentage of Golden State.
Oiler saves by stick or skate.
Yardage gained per each completion.
Top ten teams of every region.

Now I can say, "Muy bien, y Tu?"
And the first discussion, halfway through.
It makes me want to stop and holler,
"Is it just me? Or did the world get smaller?"

Missionary Limerick #2

A girl with a thick Texas drawl
Served a mission within Montreal.
Because French gave her grief,
Her discussions were brief:
"Bone Jewer. Aw Rayvore, now, y'all."

FETCH! FLIP! SCRUD!

Missionary Vocabulary and the Real World

The college professor walked up to me
And said, "Your speech is horrible.
I find your limited lexicon
Disgustingly deplorable.
Listening to you, I want to retch!"
All I could say was, "Aw, fetch."

The learned man stopped by one day.
"You ought to learn a language.
Maybe English," he snidely said,
"You could pick up some pointers in Panguitch.
I cringe with each phrase that falls from your lip."
All I could say was, "Oh, flip."

The prospective employer inspected my file.
"Everything seems in order.
We need a new man to run the whole show
North of the Mexican border.
Could be you. So speak up. And show you're no dud."
All I could say was, "Good scrud."

30

Dear John

John Jones is my name, Elder John Patrick Jones,
So when I get "Dear Johns" there are no awful
groans.

But it wasn't "Dear John" that started the letter
That caused my soul to burn.
No it wasn't "Dear John" it started, but,
"To Whom It May Concern."

All Manner of "Ites"

Go and teach the Trillobites,
The Soaringkites,
The Danskintites.
Go and teach the Megabites,
They have a lot to learn.

Go and teach the Copyrites,
The Mightymites,
The Skeeterbites.
Go and teach the Gleamingwites,
For truth they all do yearn.

But before you go, buy a book on Greek.
I heard that's what the Headlites speak.

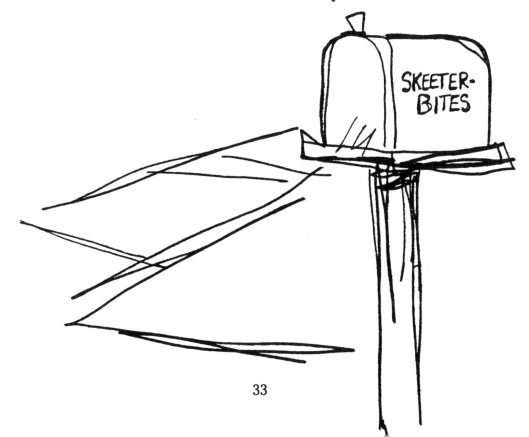

SKEETER-
BITES

Small World

One roommate went to Holland,
One roommate's in Japan.
One went to Cincinnati,
One's in the Hinterland.

We're miles apart,
But we're close as can be;
We're all teaching folks
From the same family.

Evening Prayers

Every night, before I sleep,
I pray for those in the Middle East.
I pray for food in Bangladesh.
I pray for rain in Marrakesh.
I pray for jobs in my hometown.
I pray for peace the whole world 'round.
I pray for those without a care.
I pray for worriers everywhere.

This seems like a lot when I kneel myself down,
But I've plenty of prayer to go around.

What a Difference!

"You've put on weight! You've gained a ton!"
That's what they said to brother one.
"You're bald! That hair! So thin, so few!"
That's what they said to brother two.

I think I know what they'll say to me,
Just look at these shoes, it's plain to see—
These triple-thick soles of Styrene Foam—
I'll be two inches shorter when I get home!

Missionary Limerick #3

Wrote a son, from a far away land,
"This dang language I can't understand!
It'd be easy except
Here they read right to left,
Out it figured quite haven't I and!"

Pros and Cons

I left behind:
    A mom who cooks
    A paying job
    Adventure books
    A pretty girl
    A weekly date
    My old guitar
    And sleeping late

And in return I get:
    Long hours
    Stomach flu
    Glares and glowers
    Blistered feet
    Beds with fleas
    Front door slams
    Calloused knees

The world sees this quite narrowly
And says I've made a poor decision.
Me, I take the blinders off,
And catch the peripheral vision.

Gratitude

When a kind señor points out the way,
"Muchas Gracias" is what you say.
When a Frenchman says, "Sit down and stay,"
"Merci Beaucoup" is what you say.
When you finally reach the end of day,
And your body's weary, and your mood is gray,
When you fall upon your knees to pray,
"Many Thanks" is what you say.

A Letter Home on Hump Day

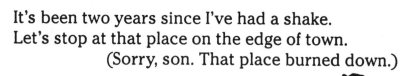

Hump Day! Hump Day!
Click your heels and jump day!

Now that I am halfway through,
I'll list the things I want to do
Upon that great and glorious morn
When from the airplane I am borne
On shoulders of the friends I've missed.
Enough of that. Now here's my list:

It's been two years since I've had a shake.
Let's stop at that place on the edge of town.
        (Sorry, son. That place burned down.)

I've pedaled a bike for twenty-four months.
So please bring my '66 mustang ragtop.
        (Uh . . . sorry, bro. It's in the shop.)

The mail's all screwed up here. I've not heard from
Jane,
So bring her. We'll hug and we'll kiss, shout, and sing!
        (Sorry, Jim. Wanna see my ring?)

Last of all, I've missed my friends
And family. I want handshakes from me to you.
        (Sorry, Jim. Think hugs will do?)

MY ELDER! WHAT A LOVELY PHOTOGRAPH. I WOULD THINK IT WOULD REALLY BOTHER YOU THAT YOUR GORGEOUSLY BEAUTIFUL GIRLFRIEND IS SEEN HERE WITH SOMEONE ELSE WHO IS OBVIOUSLY NOT HER BROTHER, AND YET QUITE CLOSE, BUT YOU SEEM TO BE TAKING IT ALL VERY WELL.
ELDER? ELDER?

It Takes Two to Tango

Mary, Mary, quite contrary
Why does your Elder groan?
You sent him your picture, the one from the prom,
And you didn't go alone.

The Mural

My first companion, Elder Brown,
Taught me Spanish and two good coin tricks.
My next companion, Elder Gray,
Proved that sleeping and teaching don't mix.
My third companion, Elder White,
Was holy and pious and stern.
My fourth companion, Elder Redd,
Kept saying, "Some day you'll learn!"

Now I'm a senior. I have Elder Green.
He's quiet. He's humble. He's grateful. He's clean.

My mission is a mural painted on a two-year wall.
My companions are the artists, leaving colors as they fall
Behind me, soon to be a brief and distant moment in my past.
Years from now, of all those colors, which ones will really last?

Health Benefits

The first thing I got in the Mission Home
Was a little yellow card.
"Gamma Globulin Record Chart"
It said. Can't be too hard
To take a shot in the rear every two or three months.
I know just what I'll do!
Each companion I get will give me a shot,
Then sign in Column Two!
When my time is up and I go home,
I'll have, for all to see,
A record of my hygiene, *and*
A Mission Pedigree!
Not only that, but I then can prove,
Should anyone care to check,
That of all those dear companions,
Not one was a pain in the neck!

Missionary Limerick #4

Now Ammon, while king's flocks he tended,
Cut off arms of the thieves that offended.
The result was conversions
And many immersions,
Though nowadays it's not recommended.

Mission Christmas Blues

It's Christmas in the mission field,
I'm feeling kind of blue.
I miss my Mom, I miss my Dad,
I miss the presents, too.
I miss the ton of greeting cards
Taped to the entry door.
I miss the way the neighbor kids
Sang "Come Let Us Adore."
I miss the bowls of candy that
Were magically refilled.
I miss the perfect yule-log fire
That only Dad could build.

But if some heav'nly angel type
Appeared and made me choose:
No missin' or no mission, well,
I'd take the Christmas Blues.

The Mission President Likens the Scriptures Unto Himself

Feet of clay don't bother me,
Nor legs of iron and stone.
It's this middle of Goodyear rubber
And this head of polished chrome.

Remember Who You Are

District Conference again,
That confusing time when
The metaphors fly thick and fast.
When what you are
Depends, so far,
On who got up and spoke last.

First, Sister Simms
Said we're all violins
Cradled in the Master's hand.
Then Elder Stone,
In a cosmic tone,
Claimed we're nothing but specks of sand.

Next Elder Kent,
With artistic bent,
Said the mission's a stage, we're the players.
And the President said,
"Without works, faith is dead,
So what are you? Doers or sayers?"

So, at this time,
I guess that I'm
A microscopic fiddle
Who hams his way
Through a two-year play,
Always talking, but doing little.

Stage Fright

When I was seven, I played a shepherd.
The Christmas show was well attended.
I had one line. My brain forgot it.
I recalled it once the play had ended.

It's been twelve years, I'm a shepherd
again,
Though now the crowds are small and few.
I learned some lines. My brain forgets them.
So the ones my heart invents will do.

Missionary Limerick #5

One young man, who was called to São Paulo,
Got this news, from a voice grim and hollow:
"I heard, down there, how
They eat stomach of cow."
He replied, "I find that hard to swallow."

He Didn't Agree with Them

It was Mormon night at the cannibal feast,
They were dining on elder stew.
The eaters were having a glorious time,
At least for an hour or two.

Then they all jumped up in a retching throng
And puked in the bushes around.
"It's not my fault," said the cannibal cook,
"You just can't keep a good man down!"

Mom's Advice Before Leaving

Life's road is hard, strewn with rocks, tears, and pain.
Wear good shoes in sunshine, galoshes in rain.

MIND YOUR MANNERS. BRUSH YOUR TEETH.
MAKE SURE TO EAT YOUR VEGETABLES.
TSK, TSK, LOOK AT THE SHINE ON
THOSE SHOES. DON'T SLOUCH...

The Voice of Experience

The Mission President, recently called,
Wrote the outgoing one a letter.
"I want to be a strong leader, like you.
How can I prepare myself better?"

MISSION PRESIDENT

AFTER

A week went by. The letter came,
Words of wisdom the new man should keep:
"You've got two months 'til you take my place.
If I were you, I'd sleep."

Midnight Snack

The other night I tossed and turned,
Asleep upon my bed.
The gargoyles of the night had come
To dance inside my head.
This evil and malicious seed
They planted in my dreams:
The cooking chores for one whole week
Controlled by Elder Weems!

I sat in chains before the feast
My "brother" had prepared.
He eyed me as I fought my bonds.
He knew that I was scared.
He shoved a plate beneath my nose
And grinned an evil grin,
"This feast was made with you in mind,
Please don't mind me, dig in!"

I coughed and gagged and shuddered
At what met my frightened eyes:
A green and greasy mound of meat
He called the "Weems Surprise."
He served it with the Soup du Jour,
Which was a Soup du Sludge.
I said it looked like thirty-weight.
He shrugged, "You be the judge."

A plate of onion muffins
With some thick potato jam.
A pitcher of some beverage
Made from celery and spam.
A peanut butter meatloaf
With some Cool Whip on the side.
A boiled and deviled egg that had
Committed suicide.

"No more!" I screamed, and found myself
Once more upon my bed,
Sitting there and shaking out
The gargoyles from my head.
My mouth was dry, but sweat poured down
My face and neck in streams.
"What's up? Another nightmare?"
Said the kindly Elder Weems.

"Now just relax. Breathe in, breathe out,"
He coaxed a soothing mood.
"You know, I'll bet you're hungry!
I'll go whip us up some food!"

The First Fast Sunday in the MTC

We went from that meeting, out the door,
With filled hearts, but stomachs bereft.
Then we spotted the sign someone taped to the wall:
"Only 23 Fast Sundays left!"

Missionary Limerick #6

A lazy young Elder named Sam
Made a spiritual turnaround. Wham!

Said the rest, one and all,
"This reminds us of Paul."
So he's called nowadays Elder Pam.

The Terror of the Tabernacle

"The Terror of the Tabernacle," such a silly thing
To call a meek and humble man like me. I don't know what could bring
The members here attending Conference to give an usher such a name.
I guess, that is, it's possible, that they don't like my game.
See, I like to have stake presidents all sitting on one pew.
It makes things much more orderly. My record's ninety-two.

A Poem for Those in Withdrawal

The best food nature can endow?
    Ice Cream!
The greatest gift to man, from cow?
    Ice Cream!
What hits the taste buds with a *pow*?
What makes the tonsils sing out, "Wow?"
What can't you get where I'm at now?
    Ice Cream!

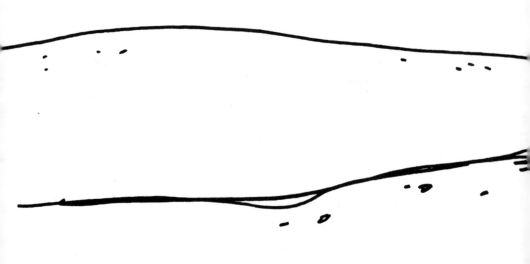

A Dear John to Ponder

"The glory of God is intelligence."
I'm sure that this is true.
But what did she mean when she wrote to me:
"I'm too glorious for you."

Bloom Where You Are Planted

If I had been a missionary in the days of yore,
I would have been at Alma's side, preaching evermore.
I would have drawn my strength from him,
He would have been my light.
With Alma as companion,
I'd have fought the glorious fight.

But here I am in modern day, in modern tie and shirt.
No Alma for companion, just a guy from Price named Burt.
But who's to say that there won't be,
A thousand years from now,
Some young galactic Elder
With a furrow in his brow,
And a sour disposition,
And a spirit full of hurt,
'Cause he could have been a stalwart
Had he served with Elder Burt.

Missionary Limerick #7

A family, by last name of Newman,
Liked to show off their gospel acumen.
Each baby that came
Got a scriptural name.
So there's Nephi, and Sam, and Kishkumen.

KISHKUMEN

A Simple Rule

"One last thing," my father said, "before you go away;
A simple rule, that if well learned will cause success each day:
Treat everyone—adult and child—as if you're in their debt,
But never once expect the same from anyone you've met."

Lament of a Music Major in a Two-elder Town

A heavenly choir awaits me when I reach my final rest;
A multitude of angels, all white and brightly dressed.
I'll lead that glorious chorus, and the heavens will stand agog!
For now, it's just three ladies, my companion, and a dog.

It Helps To Be Ignorant of Some Things

The Mission President called me in.
He said, "How did you do it?
When I assigned you Elder Scuzz
It'd last two days, I knew it!
But now it's gone for several months!
I just can't fathom how
You changed the man, like night to day!
Tell me your secret now.
He was one of the worst, a lazy oaf
Who did nothing but sleep and eat and loaf!
Nobody liked getting stuck with this bird!"
I honestly said, "I hadn't heard."

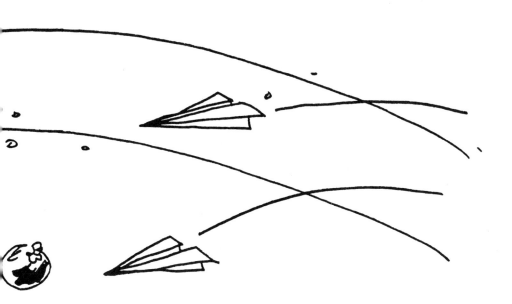

A Lesson From the Past

Samuel was a Lamanite who stood upon a wall.
The arrows flew, but not one stuck. His faith was more than all.

I stand, exposed, for two long years. Afflictions fly my way.
But none will stick, because I've learned to read and fast and pray.

Two Little Elders

This little Elder went to Iceland.
This little Elder went to Guam.
This little Elder here is freezing.
This little Elder here is wuam.

Both little Elders cried, "YIPPEEYIPPEEYIPPEE"
All the way home.

Accountability

"Who's responsible?" asked the man
Who lived next door, and in his hand
He held my errant baseball, and
I swallowed hard and said, "I am."

"Who's responsible?" screamed Coach Lee
When the other team went up by three
'Cause I lost my man inside the key.
Head bowed, I stammered, "It was me."

"Who's responsible?" Elder Ford
Smiled, looking at the week's report,
"You've made great strides, across the board!"
I answered him, "It was the Lord."

I was given, when I died,
All that the Father had. I cried,
"Why this for me?" He smiled with pride.
"You are responsible," He replied.

BRUCE CALL

ABOUT THE AUTHOR

Bruce Call works as a writer, producer, and director for Battlecreek Film & Video, a production company based in Pleasant Grove, Utah. His national award-winning work has taken him all over the U.S., the Caribbean, and Africa.

In creating this collection, Bruce drew on his own missionary experiences, having served in the Costa Rica San Jose mission.

VAL CHADWICK BAGLEY